**21st Century Junior Library**

# Ankylosaurus

*by Lucia Raatma*

CHERRY LAKE PUBLISHING * ANN ARBOR, MICHIGAN

Published in the United States of America by Cherry Lake Publishing
Ann Arbor, Michigan
www.cherrylakepublishing.com

Content Adviser: Gregory M. Erickson, PhD, Dinosaur Paleontologist,
Department of Biological Science, Florida State University, Tallahassee, Florida

Reading Adviser: Marla Conn, Read with Me Now

Photo Credits: Cover, ©RDK Photography/Alamy; page 4, ©Catmando/Shutterstock, Inc.; page 6,
©Andreas Meyer/Shutterstock, Inc.; page 8, ©claude thibault/Alamy; page 10, ©iStockphoto.com
/Syldavia; page 12, ©leonello calvetti/Shutterstock, Inc.; page 14, ©Linda Bucklin/Shutterstock, Inc.;
page 16, ©thatsmymop/Shutterstock, Inc.; page 18, ©iStockphoto.com/Andrew_Howe; page 20,
©Kumar Sriskandan/Alamy

**LIBRARY OF CONGRESS CATALOGING-IN-PUBLICATION DATA**
Raatma, Lucia.
 Ankylosaurus/by Lucia Raatma.
    p. cm.—(21st century junior library) (Dinosaurs)
 Includes bibliographical references and index.
 ISBN 978-1-61080-461-5 (lib. bdg.)—ISBN 978-1-61080-548-3 (e-book)—
ISBN 978-1-61080-635-0 (pbk.)
 1. Ankylosaurus—Juvenile literature. I. Title.
 QE862.O65R327 2013
 567.915—dc23                                    2012001922

Cherry Lake Publishing would like to acknowledge the work of
The Partnership for 21st Century Skills.
Please visit www.21stcenturyskills.org for more information.

Printed in the United States of America
Corporate Graphics Inc.
July 2012
CLFA11

# CONTENTS

The *Ankylosaurus* died out millions of years ago.

# What Was an Ankylosaurus?

**P**icture a huge dinosaur that looked like it was covered in **armor**. That's the *Ankylosaurus*. This creature lived about 70 million to 65 million years ago. It was found in what is now western North America. Today, all types of dinosaurs are **extinct**.

The *Tyrannosaurus rex* was a fierce predator.

The name *Ankylosaurus* is a Greek word meaning "**fused** lizard." The *Ankylosaurus* was mostly a peaceful animal. However, it had to protect itself from larger dinosaurs. One of its **predators** was the dangerous *Tyrannosaurus rex*. The *T. rex* was a **carnivore**.

**Make a Guess!**

How would North America's forests have looked 65 million years ago? Think about all the animals and plants that lived there. What animals were in danger? What animals were the predators?

Plates covered almost all of an
*Ankylosaurus's* body.

# What Did an *Ankylosaurus* Look Like?

The *Ankylosaurus*'s skin was made of thick oval scales. The scales covered plates of bone. These plates were hard and strong. They made the dinosaur look almost like an armored tank. The *Ankylosaurus* even had plates over its eyes for protection.

Spikes added extra protection against enemies.

The *Ankylosaurus* had large horns on its head. Rows of spikes ran along the sides of its body. Its tail was also covered in hard plates. These tail plates were fused together. This made the tail look like a giant club.

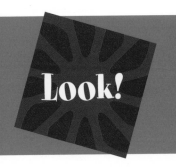

**Look!**

Have you ever been to a zoo? Next time you go, look at the animals with horns. Are some horns short? Are some long? What do the animals use their horns for?

The *Ankylosaurus* was large and strong.

The average *Ankylosaurus* was about 25 feet (7.6 meters) long. This bulky dinosaur could weigh as much as 4 tons. That makes it one of the heaviest dinosaurs that ever lived. How much is 4 tons? It's about the same as two cars.

The *Ankylosaurus* was as tall as some adult people.

Like an armored tank, the *Ankylosaurus* sat low to the ground. It was about 6 feet (1.8 m) wide. Yet it was only 5.5 feet (1.7 m) tall. It had four short legs and a short neck. The *Ankylosaurus* had a long body. But its head and teeth were small.

**Create!** Draw a picture of an army tank. Then draw a picture of an *Ankylosaurus*. What do they have in common?

The *Ankylosaurus* stayed where there
was plenty of food.

# How Did an *Ankylosaurus* Live?

The *Ankylosaurus* was an **herbivore**. It ate only plants. It took a lot to feed such a big dinosaur! The *Ankylosaurus* was a slow-moving creature. Scientists think it spent its days in forests. It probably stayed along rivers and lakes. There, it **grazed** among the grasses, trees, and other plants.

An *Ankylosaurus* could use its tail to hit predators.

An *Ankylosaurus* had to stay on the lookout. It was always in danger from other dinosaurs. But the *Ankylosaurus* could protect itself. It would swing its huge tail like a baseball bat. Its only weak spot was its belly. This was not covered in plates. Predators had to flip the *Ankylosaurus* over to attack it.

**Think!**

What other animals are covered with hard material for protection? Can you think of other ways animals use their bodies in defense?

Scientists carefully clean and study fossils.

How do we know about the *Ankylosaurus*? Scientists have learned about this dinosaur by studying its **fossils**. Some were discovered in Alberta, Canada. Others were found in Montana and Wyoming in the United States. These fossils are displayed at the American Museum of Natural History. This museum is in New York City, New York.

**Ask Questions!**

Have you ever visited a science museum? Were there any dinosaur fossils there? Ask museum workers about how dinosaurs lived and died. Your teacher will have some answers, too!

# GLOSSARY

**armor** (AR-mur) protective scales, bones, and spines that cover some animals

**carnivore** (KAHR-nuh-vor) an animal that eats meat

**extinct** (ek-STINGKT) describing a type of plant or animal that has completely died out

**fossils** (FAH-suhlz) the preserved remains of living things from thousands or millions of years ago

**fused** (FYOOZD) joined together

**grazed** (GRAYZD) fed on low-growing plants

**herbivore** (HUR-buh-vor) an animal that eats plants rather than other animals

**predators** (PRED-uh-turz) animals that live by hunting other animals for food

# FIND OUT MORE

## BOOKS

Gray, Susan Heinrichs. *Ankylosaurus*. Mankato, MN: The Child's World, 2010.

Rockwood, Leigh. *Ankylosaurus*. New York: PowerKids Press, 2012.

## WEB SITES

### American Museum of Natural History: Fossil Halls

*www.amnh.org/exhibitions/ permanent/fossils*
Learn about the two dinosaur halls at this museum.

### National Geographic Kids: Ankylosaurus

*http://kids.nationalgeographic. com/kids/animals/creaturefeature/ ankylosaurus-magniventris*
Get the facts about the armor-plated *Ankylosaurus*.

# INDEX

## ABOUT THE AUTHOR

Lucia Raatma has written dozens of books for young readers. She and her family live in the Tampa Bay area of Florida. They enjoy looking at the dinosaur fossils at the local science museum.